waterways series

Krapp's Last Tape — The Musical

releasing new voices, revealing new perspectives

Krapp's Last Tape — The Musical

waterways
an imprint of flipped eye publishing
www. flippedeye.net

First Edition
Copyright © Peter Ebsworth, 2016
Cover Image © Jeff Hutchinson, 2014
Cover Design © flipped eye publishing, 2016

Thanks are due to the editors of the following publications, in which many of these poems, or earlier versions of them, first appeared: Brittle Star, Connections (Kent), The Delinquent, Equinox, Fin, 14 Magazine, The Frogmore Papers, The Interpreter's House, Iota, Magma, The Morning Star, The New Statesman, Obsessed With Pipework, Orbis, Other Poetry, Poetry Monthly, Poetry Nottingham, South, The Spectator, Lunar Poetry, Prole, Trespass and Under the Radar. ' A Certain Knowledge' was joint first prize-winner in the 2011 Crystal Palace Festival Competition.

ISBN-978-1-905233-43-4
Editorial work for this series is supported by the Arts Council of England

Supported using public funding by
ARTS COUNCIL
LOTTERY FUNDED **ENGLAND**

This book is dedicated to the extended Ebsworth and Everitt families, as well as the singer songwriter Tim Hardin 1941-1980, and the playwright Sarah Kane 1971-1999, both of whom left us too early.

Krapp's Last Tape – The Musical

Acknowledgements

Over the last several years I have received help from many people in seeking both to write poetry and read it well in public. They are too numerous to name, but I would like to thank Karen Annesen, Kathryn Maris, Simon Barraclough and especially Niall O'Sullivan and John Stammers, who have also given early and continuing support to my efforts in publishing and editing South Bank Poetry magazine, since I initially floated the idea and then published the first issue in June 2008. Editing three issues a year of SBP has certainly influenced my own poetry. I am also grateful for the work that Sara Nesbitt contributed during her period as Assistant Editor and the input and advice of my good friend, and now publisher and co-editor of SBP, Katherine Lockton. Thanks also to Ely Ahamed, Mya, and all of the staff at the Poetry Cafe for providing a friendly atmosphere in which poetry can thrive. Finally, I must mention the Forest Poets Stanza group I belong to. Always superbly organised and run by Paul McGrane and Michael Sims, the advice and support of its members is invariably helpful, enjoyable and productive.

Krapp's Last Tape — The Musical

Contents

Sooner Than You Think	.11
Look-alike	.12
Pythagoras Prepares His Troops	.13
The Goat	.14
The Unexpected Elevation of the Online Shoebox and its Consequences	.15
Sawdust Memories	.16
Two Winters	.17
Playing at Being Homeless	.19
Listening to Sergeant Pepper	.21
The Very Brief Rise and Fall of Andy the Amoeba and his Contribution to Popular Music in the Late 1960s	.22
The Infinite Variety of the Music Accompanying Silence	.23
The Four Board Rubbers of the Apocalypse	.24
Modigliani Returns with a Chinese Takeaway	.25
Oral History from the Mediatheque at the National Film Theatre	.26
Boomer Noir	.27
I Could Tell You About Unrequited Love but I'd Rather Discuss the Ballet	.29
At the End of An Opera	.30
Krapp's Last Tape - The Musical	.31
The Empathy of the Critic	.34
The Playwright Sarah Kane's Literary Agent Recalls Their Last Meetings on the tenth Anniversary of Her Death	.35
Iago Is My Hero	.36

Staged .37
Observations on Vicky Leyton's Recent Legal Triumph
in Benidorm, Which Allows her to Resume Performing
under the Stage Name of Sticky Vicky .38
Paper Doom .39
Amid the turbulence .40
The Exchange .41
Red Bottle .42
At a Paris Café, 1925 .43
also unknown as .44
Marlon Brando Decides to Set up a Nationwide Chain of Car
Parks and Addresses Potential Franchisees .46
Tony Soprano Sums Things up and Consults his Therapist
for the Last Time .47
Serial Killer e Pena di Morte at the Museo Criminale, Florence .48
The Girl with the Lobster Tattoo .49
There Are Other Ways of Removing a Tattoo .50
The Narcissism of Small Differences .51
Blithe Spirits .52
The Launch of a Thousand .53
Sing a song of sex pants .54
The Absence of Magic .55
A Certain Knowledge .56
Ending .57
Only Once .58
Reflections at Samos Harbour .60
Accumulation in the Tivoli Gardens .61

Sooner Than You Think

It is late summer on the train home,
and opposite, an old man is prepared
for every cold spell which could arrive.
A cloth cap, an overcoat, a smart striped
shirt buttoned up to the top and something
extra in maroon, tucked under his trousers.

I find his boy scout senility touching.
This may seem too harsh a word,
although I do not intend it as a jibe,
having already experienced
what it means to unpack the shopping
and put toilet rolls in the fridge.

I arrive back at my flat
and, while fixing myself a drink,
drop my only ice cube
onto the kitchen floor.
I rinse it under the cold tap.
Carelessly it disappears.

Look-alike

Used to dye my hair, then stopped
when it became a whiter shade of grey
and I realised I could be a Paul Newman look-alike.
Not the Paul Newman of *Somebody Up There Likes Me*
in the sweetness of his youth, Brick on a hot tin roof
or even the right wing radio jock in *WUSA* .

For me it has to be the much older Newman,
playing the gangster in *The Road To Perdition,*
who scowls the Tom Hanks anti-hero in the eye:
tells him, *You and I both have done things which
mean that if there is a hell we shall be going there.*

I could manage that look, speak those words,
wear contacts a brighter blue than my eyes,
play the role, grow into it, maybe even get
to have my very own brand of salad cream.
But if you laugh at me I will follow and kill you.

Pythagoras Prepares His Troops

If you're going into battle,
you have to get the angles right.
To be ready, there has to be
a burn rising slowly,
from the stomach to the throat,
where it's corked back down
so your chest silently throbs
alongside your heartbeat.
Your wrists and fingers
are all calm, as alert
and focused as your eyes.

You aim where you have to.
Try and get your shot in first
and, most important of all,
remember:
a target has no widow,
a target has no mother,
brother, sister or lover.
And when the battle's over,
you can sing old familiar songs
to help you get back to sleep,
wherever your head is resting.

The Goat

My grandfather, Francis Audley Ebsworth,
drank two bottles of Johnnie Walker a day
and his two grocer's shops into the ground.
He blamed his chronic drinking
on being gassed.

If they'd had a really good week's takings
at the one in the Walworth Road,
he'd announce, *We're off to Norfolk!*
Then he and my dad
would cab it all the way there.

Sometimes, before he blacked out,
Francis Audley would tell his son
how he had to take breaks and piss on
his machine gun to cool it down
before he could *kill more of the Hun.*

At home they kept a goat
who'd eat anything, including newspapers.
One day, approaching middle age,
he ate a Daily Express too many
and his stomach exploded.

The Unexpected Elevation of the Online Shoebox and its Consequences

After the over-communication wars
broke out, everything was finished.
Books, journals, manuscripts, gone
long before, the way of all hard copy
when few thought it feasible to construct
somewhere to deposit the old and unwanted,
let alone face onscreen total wipeout,
with the Online Shoebox being the only
survivor in the cyber bunker.

In the Shoebox's Black Museum,
there are torn images
of matted dead flowers taped to railings,
surrounded by soft toy animals
and dolls, misshapen and degraded,
evidence how horrible things
have happened to infants, at a time
later than anyone could have imagined.

Sawdust Memories

I grew up on red meat, lots of it,
refusing bread or crisps, even sausages,
often sharing weekday lunch
with mum *and* dad, because he left
for work in Smithfield at 3 AM
and was usually home around noon.
Sawdust, a constant stowaway,
accumulated in trousers' turn-ups,
imbued with blood and fat:
the sweet smell of the afterdeath.
Then the promotions, indoor jobs,
the transatlantic phone deals
for turkeys by the hundred thousands,
regular hours and retirement.
His turn-ups had become cleaner
and were frequently out of fashion.
The men who'd worked in the meat trade
still met up at boxing dinners
a couple of times a year.
They sat together and ate at tables
around the ring, before the final course
of bouts, sawdust and the rest;
served by the bell.

Two Winters

The first day I did a paper round
coincided with the beginning
of the great British winter of 1962-63.
I'd agreed to do it as a one-off
for my friend Jon who wouldn't be back
from relatives until the day after Boxing Day.
As it was a Sunday, extra pay was the clincher;
although I hadn't anticipated how heavy
the bags would be with the papers' supplements
or the problem of keeping them dry.
Despite the newsagent explaining the route,
it took me six hours and I went home frozen.
My family were worried and Dad
had been out looking for me on foot.

In January I decided if I couldn't beat it
I'd stay local and try snow clearing,
knocking on people's doors and shovelling
it off their paths for a shilling or two.
This generally worked fine
with enough takers willing to pay my rate,
except for a misunderstanding with a pensioner
who thought it was free when I'd meant
half-price. I confess that I shovelled
some of the snow back onto her drive.

In 1976, I spent Christmas in Buffalo with friends.
Was there when Sarah, the youngest of the Chisolms,
found out what happened to a school friend of hers.
He'd been drinking along the Elmwood Avenue Strip
on Christmas Eve and tried to walk home in a blizzard.
Must have fallen asleep in a drift, as he was discovered
the next morning, face down in a clearing by a lake.
As the snow melted and he was turned over
on the grass, water ran down his cheeks.

Playing at Being Homeless

Friends, Mods, fifteen or sixteen years old,
at seaside towns on bank holiday weekends
with no thought for where we'd sleep: our
money already stretched for meals, fags, coffees.
Chasing rockers through Dreamland in Margate,
never fighting yet lapping it up.
Seafront summer time, always cold after dark,
bus shelters became our night shelters.
In Clacton, two blokes in their twenties
took pity, let us in their caravan.
Nothing dodgy, unlike the man we hitched
a ride to Hastings with. We followed sand dunes
to a cave and hid there for the night. Woke
needing to scratch and saw insects all around us.

My best friend Kevin was with me
and again in Folkestone, listening to Soul
and Motown on the jukebox at The Acropolis,
the top Mod coffee bar in the South East.
A couple of doors down was a fish and chip shop
run by a chainsmoker in his sixties. Late at night,
he scraped up some fish he'd dropped
on the floor, re-dipped it in sizzling fat,
placed it with the freshly fried ones.
Witnesses, he let us stay upstairs.
The next day, we discovered we'd been sleeping
close by several men in their thirties and forties,
who got out of bed wearing grubby vests
and pants. We dressed quickly and left.
On the mile walk to The Singing Kettle,
Kev mentioned he'd failed to find the toilet
in the dark, so conducted a muffled piss
into a sack of potatoes. We both had egg
and chips at the caff, washed down with tea.

Listening to Sergeant Pepper

at Laura's house
soon after its release

the same side playing
over and over again

we'd just worked our
way round to doing more

when moan
turned to groan

as I was shook out
she thought

she'd heard her mother
coming down the stairs

to *She's leaving home*
and I wished it had already happened

The Very Brief Rise and Fall of Andy the Amoeba and his Contribution to Popular Music in the Late 1960s

Allegedly, Andy was the one who inspired
The Incredible String Band's cellular song.
His laidback aimless demeanour
in keeping with the Zeitgeist of 1968.
But even as The Incredibles
were performing at The London Palladium,
Andy was breathing his last down a drain
on nearby Great Marlborough Street,
pursued by a phalanx of jealous Hydras
singing, *You're not slithering anymore*
and he expired to their chant of *...and you*
haven't got two cells to rub together.

The Infinite Variety of the Music Accompanying Silence

A musician I met in Turkey
was vehement in his opinion
that John Cage's silent composition
4' 33" can be played well or badly.
I found his viewpoint persuasive,
so now, when I go to the toilet,
I concentrate on the second hand
of my watch as it goes around
and listen to every single one
of the chamber's background sounds:
for as Heraclitus says in his collected fragments,
you never hear the same penny spent twice.

The Four Board Rubbers of the Apocalypse

was my first sculpture,
done as a joke
before I took a year off work.

Put together on the shelf
above my desk, I placed two flat,
next to each other
but not touching; the third I put
on top of and across the fourth,
leaving a slightly bigger space
separating both from
the first and second ones.

I began to enjoy looking at them,
especially the way their neatness
arranged in the space
contrasted with my messy desk.

Asked people to look after it
while I was away.
When I returned,
one of the board rubbers had gone.
Something was missing.

Modigliani Returns with a Chinese Takeaway

Suggested by Modigliani's Female Nude, around 1916, the Courtauld Gallery

I found her eyes closed
just as I'd left them
and her breasts, relaxed,
looked neither big or small;
nothing to suggest imminent consummation
or even the foreplay of dim sum.
I enjoyed using chopsticks,
instead of paint brushes, as I traced
up from the shadow on her inside thigh,
air-picked her brown lipped
belly button, then moved back down
to contemplate with playful intent,
the forked wisp of her dark hair.

Oral History from the Mediatheque at the National Film Theatre

My second visit there I chose to watch
a 1990 Documentary, *The Blitz: Fifty Years On.*
Listened to Ray, a retired electrician, recall how bad
it was with Hitler's bombs destroying houses,
people he knew being killed, his sheltering down
the Underground and going hungry. After the war
there were still shortages, although he was lucky -
having a trade and family. From the mid-1950s
things got a lot better, as painful memories were
replaced with nostalgia. His mate Stan chipped in,
recounting how you could go to the pictures,
eat a Wimpy and Chips, get a shag and still have change
from a ten-bob note. For an extra shilling, Ray's sister
would wear her old gas mask while you were doing it.

Boomer Noir

I'd felt as old and out of place
as the Angus Steak House in Leicester Square,
until fifty became the new forty,
sixty became the new forty-five
and my daughter Katie joked at her fortieth party,
*Gee dad, the way things are going
you'll soon be younger than me!*
I inwardly glowed with the glamour of my new status,
licensed to look at women in the old way again,
which had to be fatal, and it was.

Julie, my mistress of thirty years ago, made contact,
*Peter, we must meet. Everything's changed.
Now the grandchildren have grown up and left home
we can soon finally be together.*
I wanted a down payment to show she meant business.
We arranged to meet in the alley
by the bottom of her south coast suburban garden.
I felt meeker soon as her lips located my big whatsit;
and as I gazed at the bobbles on her pink fluffy slippers —
he thinks I've just popped out to empty the rubbish —
she bent down again to clean me up
with a moist wipe she put into a plastic bag.

It was a nice touch and I really appreciated it,
until her husband Jim was found with his head caved in,
my DNA all over the backs of his thighs.
There was no proof I'd ever known Julie
and the judge was scathing when I denied ever meeting Jim,
telling the jury, *Everyone leads a double life these days.*

Later found out Julie used the life insurance
to move to France with a new lover.
I still had a hard spot for her, which hurt my body
as I lay on the concrete floor in the heat of the cell.
One day got an El Greco postcard with no message,
and remembered a conversation with Julie about art,
when after I'd asked what nationality he was
she'd looked at me in an unusual way.
Over the years I've thought about that a lot.

I Could Tell You About Unrequited Love but I'd Rather Discuss the Ballet

Such as the evening I took daffodils
to throw onto the stage at Covent Garden
so I could have one of those moments,
when the ballerina takes her curtain calls,
already holding the management's bouquets.
She receives a shower from The Balcony,
some landing at her feet, a couple
brushing a hip or shoulder, as she bows,
looks up and smiles just for you...

but I left the flowers in the car and I'm back
home parking in my spot, as a young woman
I've not seen before — head down, looking forlorn —
walks past just as I start to open the door.
I pick up the bunch from the back seat; think
about catching up, saying hello, presenting
her with it: although it's late, winter dark
and I might startle her. Instead, I leave them
on the passenger seat, by which time she's gone.

At the End of An Opera

for Katherine

The most I can manage is to shout Bravo!
and occasionally a tear rolls down for a favourite.

But at least I never abbreviate it to Bo
which is really pretentious, and frankly, wimpish.

Best, by far, are the whoops of women that rise
and call to each other across the auditorium,

defiant of convention in their Carmenish way,
full-throated, uninhibited, hellcattish.

Krapp's Last Tape - The Musical

Not a banana in the house
and I can't sing a note.
Never could. Always wanted to sing
but never could. Even failed in my
head. Tried and tried. Music teacher
hit me round the head for messing
around when I did my best.
Six foot seven and German, not
a tap, a clout, almost a punch
which hurt. Today he'd have been
sent to prison, then nothing. So wrote
instead, later on. These files of drafts,
attempts at lyric writing. 1993, August.
Tried to write about the one who was
the one then, who turned out to be
only the one then, not the one who
was really the one, who'd been the one
before and later would always be the one.
Turned out not even to be the one then
but did write how her absence always
surrounded me; a circle of stopped
clocks, never mended, never could be
mended, just circling,surrounding,
no change, no hope, no tick.
Another draft. 1995, September. Tania.
Makes me smile. Tania from Sao Paulo,
living in Kilburn. She had freckled breasts
I loved and, when she gave me a Bombay roll,
had a way to twist and flick me at the moment,
so my sperm would land on the sheet, not her.
Asked why she did this but she never replied

because early on she told me she was very shy,
as if saying that would serve to cover everything.
1981, March. Irene told me when we split up
how much she'd enjoyed the sex, and she had.
Yet hardly touched me there and, years later,
still wondered, if we'd done other things,
would it have gone on and been different
and maybe that was always the problem.
Was trying to find my voice then, wrote
how accidents caused the same scar in
that place on our faces but vulnerabilities
are not shared. Not lyrical, not sing song.
My scar is gone now, a white lip-line on photos.

Thank goodness that stuff about the voice is over.
Style, not the voice, is what counts.
Renewal, the new, the different.
Fashion is nothing, style is permanent.
My mother used to sing.
Not a good voice but Rosa always sang
doing the housework. Happy songs
from before the war and after.
Watched her smile and laugh
before a stranger attempted to kill her.
Rosa's screams saved her as he smashed
her head against the door and strangled
her, heard by a man walking down our road
who turned back. Patrick Inwards sent to
prison but not for long enough.
Rosa never sang again
until she was in a home, thirty seven years later.
Saw her smile and join in the hymns
as she could no longer remember.

Every good boy deserves an aberration
and sometimes I have been a good boy.
2004, broke the habit of sitting in the bar,
listening to interval comments on opening
night and sat in the stalls. Romola Garai
in *Calico*. Not just the performance.
Never seen such a beauty on stage,
and her body, naked, shone with it
the way light revealed fine hairs on legs,
arms. Best body I've ever seen, and how
she can act. Oh yes, she can act all right
and maybe she can sing as well.
I won't be leaving yet, no, not yet
closing with a yelp to providence.
Looking can be enough, remembering never is.

The Empathy of the Critic

"... and the ever gorgeous Sinead Cusack, who plays two roles."
was how I ended my splendid review of Stoppard's *Rock N Roll*,
significant also for my trademark insertion of a personal anecdote
revealing that Syd Barratt, whose figure and music loom large
in the play, didn't, as the obituaries stated, go back to live
with his mum in Cambridge after he'd cracked up,
as he'd never left home, only moved into her garage, where my
then girlfriend visited him regularly, possibly two-timing me,
but I was too thrilled by the connection to be bothered. Seeing
Sinead again, reminded me of the time I was standing outside
The Royal Court ready for the London opening of *Six Degrees
Of Separation*. Stockard Channing, divine as Betty in the film
of Grease, was the lead, and Sinead, arriving to see it, stopped
and beamed when she saw me. Now you can't beat
a late September tan and I looked wonderful. She was definitely
up for it and I seriously thought what delicious revenge I might
have on my old ex Julia if I could get inside the wife of Jeremy Irons,
then track her down and tell. Julia had confessed teenage crushes
on Royal Shakespearians but nothing Clark Gable-ish, and although
she'd enjoyed *Brideshead*, gladly skipped episodes so we could
enjoy evening romps. No. The fateful turn was a Friday matinee
showing of *The French Lieutenant's Woman* at the Beckenham Odeon.
As he loomed more unconfined than life, in a way the stage or small
screen cannot compete with, even in that average film, she was hooked
Then it was Jeremy Irons this, Jeremy Irons that, how she just 'knew'
he was a Virgo, and things were never the same again. As I said,
I'm sure Sinead was willing but I was meeting up with Isabel, and after
all, it was still Julia that I really wanted to screw.

The Playwright Sarah Kane's Literary Agent Recalls Their Last Meetings on the tenth Anniversary of Her Death

She dared me to bring her plays
about anger, justice, love and grace.
So I called her bluff: handed back
copies of *Blasted, Crave* and *Cleansed.*
She laughed, a few days after returned,
leaving her next one on my desk,
before the curtains were opened.

Iago Is My Hero

Wanted to write *IAGO IS MY HERO*
on the back of the toilet door,
though even if I had
they wouldn't necessarily know
it's not his role in the play I love most
but his creed in Otello.
When Verdi removed the *h*
the *t* became so much sharper.
If I stab you in the back,
you won't feel it until I pull the knife out:
not enough people know how to hold a grudge,
that's the trouble with the world today.

Staged

Bobbie seems like a nice girl
and wears a mini-kilt above bare legs.
As the acts come and go she smiles,
laughs, claps, in all the right places.
Her turn begins with a monologue,
full of ham emotion and non-sequiturs.
Explains she is *not a writer at all,*
does impro and a friend takes notes,
he writes up into pieces she performs.

Bobbie stays afterwards to chat and swap
names and numbers by the banisters
where the stairs meet the upstairs bar.
Walking down towards the basement
I glance leftwards and up
to check if she's a real Scotsman.
She is wearing clean, white knickers.
One disappointment after another.

Observations on Vicky Leyton's Recent Legal Triumph in Benidorm, Which Allows her to Resume Performing under the Stage Name of Sticky Vicky

I saw your 'Sexy Magic Show' only once
in 1987, yet often wondered how you've coped
with the successive enlargements of the EU
when performing your famous pulling-out-the-flags trick.
Has it been like that dissenting German general — never seen again,
who approached Hitler on the eve of battle:
Mein Fuhrer. I think it would be really awfully gemutlich
if we were to draw the line at Finland.
Or did you make them smaller
and march on to Lithuania?

O Victoria, sticky or not,
there is no shame in what you do
or the company you've kept,
but don't leave it too long, like Nureyev
booed off the stage at the Sunderland Empire
or Georgie Best not even taking a bow
that last time in the November Potteries.
Take the end of season slot at DELBOYS bar,
1a.m. Tuesday, second week of October.
Go through all your routines to applause and cheers,
squat, take off those bottle tops, cut and run.

Paper Doom

One thing I like about Benidorm at night
is the street entertainers in The Old Town:
couples in dress-up outfits
who, for a Euro or less,
come alive and dance The Charleston
or a routine copied from the silent flickers,
to some jazz-age music.

Last Sunday at eleven o'clock,
I'd just passed a jiving Travolta and Olivia,
when I saw a Grim Reaper
shrouded in black from head to toe
-not even eye slits-
carrying a wooden scythe,
its blade covered in crinkled silver.

Mentioned this to Luis, a barman
who's worked there for years.
He laughed, said *that's a new one.*
In fact, nobody admits to seeing him
and, as I'm flying home today,
keep finding myself trying to remember
whether or not he had a collection box.

Amid the turbulence

and the off-on flashes of cabin lights,
with crackle breaking into the pilot's strained tones
before the intercom cut out completely,
a meal was served.

When an elderly woman in row nine
spotted her roll bouncing along the aisle
and requested another, the stewardess snapped,
Never mind your bloody roll!
Can't you see we're in an emergency!

Those who heard
were now under no illusions
and, after the lights stopped flashing,
tried to stay calm as they finished
their supper in the dark.

The Exchange

Telegrams to and fro didn't prepare Li Cunxin
for what he'd find after he was met by English Ben.
Crackle on the intercom had surprisingly evoked
how Madam Mao's guards had twisted his limbs around
so they felt like a series of wavy lines implanted in the centre
of his pain. The voices he heard were not in his head,
they were instructions on how to dance politically,
drilled steps, so he responded as a dog to a whistle
each time he performed for the Peoples' Beijing Ballet.

The sound of the plane landing introduced freedom.
The overwhelming choices on American radio
instilled receptiveness to Ben Stevenson's choreography.
The repetition internalised in his steps was replaced
by loose-limbed, flowing movements to *Rhapsody in Blue*.
The old, tinny Gershwin recording inspired him at rehearsals,
the opening night in Houston became his first huge success.

He had been ordered not to fall in love in the West
but Li would have loved Anna, a fellow dancer in the troupe,
whatever the circumstances. It could have been the end
for Ben's exchanges with China, and though he'd
known nothing until after they were married.
Letting down Ben, Li went to the Embassy to explain
that only he should be blamed for what had happened.
They resolved to grab him on Chinese soil, so Ben,
Barbara Bush and Reagan appealed to Deng Xiao Ping.
After being released, he became Houston Ballet's
Principal dancer, his parents allowed one trip out to applaud.

Red Bottle

Tom was so anti-communist his views would have made
Joe McCarthy somersault in his grave. Unlike his great
uncle Syd, a fellow traveller who took a Progress Tour
to Moscow in the early 1950s and returned with a spring
in his heart no-one had witnessed before, although it
didn't last long. Tom learnt most of this after Syd died,
wondered if his disillusionment had been caused by
the Soviet invasion of Hungary in 1956, Kruschev's
histrionics, or perhaps the extravagance of the space
race. He was surprised Syd had appointed him executor
of his estate. In his study he discovered a box containing
the usual souvenirs, including a map of the Moscow
underground and statuette of Stalin. The only puzzle
was a red bottle, wrapped in a clean, white handkerchief;
the Russian script flaked at the edges. Tom spotted
a few drops of liquid, unscrewed the lid and sniffed.
It had a musky smell with a distinctive after-kick of almonds.
He showed the now empty bottle to an old university friend
who'd read Russian. Simon identified it as The Breath of Stalin,
a perfume produced at the height of the personality cult
in 1952. Then told Tom it was one of a special limited edition
presented to foreign visitors and that he might have had
a lucky escape. A legend has it, Stalin himself
breathed a curse into each of the bottles, swearing those
who inhaled them after his death would later have their
souls conjoined with his in an atheist hell.

At a Paris Café, 1925

Suzanne and Sophie
stopped for a drink.
Suzanne played with her coffee
and looked along the table at Sophie,
whose cassis sat untouched
while she drew a caricature
of a boss or film star.

Those were the days.
Between the wars
and before the crash.
Wearing cloche hats and smiles
in late afternoon sunshine.
The phone rang and the waiter
Jacques walked over to answer it.

He was lucky, as the motorcycle
careered past him, hitting the booth
just before he would have got there.
Packages were scattered everywhere.
As the moustached rider stumbled to his feet,
he cursed in Austrian-accented German,
making no attempt to apologise.

I know what you're thinking,
but it was no more him
than it could've been Woody Allen.
Suzanne and Sophie's dresses were soon cleaned
and they had other hats to wear;
although in later years they remained a little nervous,
so sometimes Jacques gave them a drink on the house.

also unknown as

I travel from town to town as a missing person.
Usually it's plain amnesia,
but sometimes I say I left my family
because the pressure was too great,
and I can't remember.

Once, I fell in love
and she almost persuaded me
to settle down,
get a flat,
become a Big Issue seller.

I like the attention though.
The sympathy and kindness
of the caring professionals
and ordinary members of the public.
I missed it when I had to lay low for a while,
because of that idiot on the beach
with all his labels cut out;
who wouldn't talk, yet played the piano,
going over the top,
spoiling things for the rest of us.

Been in a few scrapes.
Cuts and bruises, nothing serious.
I'm a professional,
know how to run, fall properly,
roll myself into a ball for protection.
Can't tell you the number
of cups of tea I've had in police stations.

Best of all, I like my photo
going in the local paper.
When it's printed, I move on quickly.
It's usually between the car ads
and the sports reports,
which isn't a bad place to be.
Sometimes it's in the front half,
although I can get lost there.

One August in Hull, I almost made
page three. Then a bloke living
near the railway lines forgot to draw the curtains
when he was shagging a goat.
Everyone on the three-thirty from St. Pancras
saw him, so he was banged to rights.
The psychiatrist said it was *a cry for help*.
But then with a goat, how can they tell?

Marlon Brando Decides to Set up a Nationwide Chain of Car Parks and Addresses Potential Franchisees

I wanted to be a burglar alarm installation engineer
with *Brando's* or *Marlon's* on the sides of my van,
so my Hollywood friends knew it would be me:
providing a personal service, demonstrating
how I'd finally given up all the acting stuff.
But I realised the demand would be overwhelming,
plus I like to spend time away on my atoll.
Gentlemen, I tell you these things so you will not think
I have come to these decisions lightly, without
consideration of all the possibilities that can happen.
I am willing to make two thirty second commercials
which would be shown on national networks.
These car parks would not require the blood, sweat and beers
of Stanley Kowalski or Terry Molloy's noble but dumbass guts.
This project requires the high tone of my Mark Anthony
which was not outshone by James Mason's Brutus; or better,
the clipped vowels of Fletcher Christian and good manners
and humility of whoever the fuck I was in *Teahouse Moon.*
This should guarantee regular customers in our concrete paradises,
otherwise we will become solely dependent on passing trade,
the desperation of strangers, a situation which even the occasional
cameo and intervention by myself will not retrieve, as weeds
grow through the concrete surrounded by the abandoned
and our lots' hearts shall become darkness on each day we see.

Tony Soprano Sums Things up and Consults his Therapist for the Last Time

It was never the fucking way
they said it was before.
Like the posing in the movies
when they stood and said,
It's not personal, it's business.
The fuck it isn't personal!
We learned this shit from the Romans!
It's always been very fucking personal.
Even my dear old mama,
God rest her scheming soul,
could tell you that.
Sure, I have a voice which launched
a thousand hits, but it don't make me a fucking
icon for just showing up and doing my job.

Jennifer. Doctor. I have this real fucking
bitch of a dream, if you'll pardon
my misogyny but it's been a bad fucking day.
I have this repeating dream
where I've got off a flight
and they've taken me into a side room.
I've been strip searched before
but nothing like this.
Instead of the surgical glove and the Vaseline
there are two big fucking sets of Eagles' talons
and they claw deep up inside.

Serial Killer e Pena di Morte *at the Museo Criminale, Florence*

Picked her up outside the museum, around
the corner from Michaelangelo's David.
She'd been captivated by the life-size
Charles Manson waxwork beaming out at her.
Well, you mustn't let LIFE get you down
was my opening line, which I followed
with an account of having known
members of The Process, a London-based
cult with links to the Manson family.

She was enthralled. They always are.
No matter the degree of separation
from your contact with the kills,
the remotest connection's enough
to produce goose bumps on
the skin of a serial murderer groupie.

In the Hotel del Nazioni she laughed a lot
at pillow talk of how huge the model
for The David must have been.
Imagine chopping that fucker into pieces
and dropping them off around the city!
But what made her really sizzle
between the legs, was when I confessed
that, much as I enjoy hotels, I miss
the comfort of knowing whoever shares
my bed, jugs of acid in my bathroom
are never more than six feet away.

The Girl with the Lobster Tattoo

There wasn't much light,
so he didn't notice it
until she got on top of him,
and only after his *petit mort*
left them slightly apart –
taking a breather and each other in –
did he venture a closer look.

Above her left breast,
at first glance it seemed amateurish,
in places the ink was not joined up.
He amused himself with the notion
it was a long shrimp or small lobster,
yes, definitely a lobster,
you could tell by the tail.

She'd been in a good mood
until he teased her about it,
now pointing at the tattoo,
declared she was a Scorpio.
As he turned towards the curtains,
head bowed, the tail's shadow grew huge.
When he felt her touch again,
his body went numb, his breath stilled.

There Are Other Ways of Removing a Tattoo

She stood there naked
and said: What do you think?
It'd been two years since I'd seen her
and didn't want to say the wrong thing,
which can have consequences
even if you comment on a top;
cosmetic surgery is much more serious.
So I just ummed and oohed, then tried
to stare in a positive approving way.
Oh no! Nothing's been done to my boobs,
she said, laughing,
so I knew my wordless diplomacy succeeded.
Took me on a tour of her knees, stomach and thighs.
In Argentina the prices are much cheaper
and she'd got a great deal.
Her tattoo had gone when the lipo was done.
She'd never liked it much anyway,
I remembered the devil's face, his little fork.

The Narcissism of Small Differences

Eric told the king he had not brought figs to win his daughter's hand, but promised they'd honeymoon in Trieste and, as James Joyce had done, breakfast every day on *presnitz* and red wine at the Pasticceria Pirona. Eric wasn't only thinking of her health in bringing dates instead; remembered Christmas as a child when figs always came plain, stuck together in a cellophane covered slab. He was won over by the presentation of the dates in their special, picture box; the presence of the stone in each one giving pause for thought and restraint. The King's daughter's insatiable appetite for figs disturbed him and he believed the substitution of dates for figs had the potential to negate the aversion therapy favoured by her father. Eric explained he didn't find big women unattractive. In fact, he was very desirous of Miranda off the telly, whom he thought could give him satisfaction; any clumsiness compensated for by enthusiasm and a minesweeper tongue, although he recognised there would be differences between Miranda the character and Miranda the actress, fantasy not being confined to fairy tales. So he asked the king if he might try the dates alternative on his daughter and could he please suspend the other tasks and trials? He had the wand, given to him by the stranger to whom he had been kind and trusted, to tap and refill the bowl of dates. He hoped he'd not need it, that the aunt would come across the sea on her own accord. And that the three hares would not be disturbed and distressed by magical manoeuvres before they were dispatched and prepared for the feast.

Blithe Spirits

Thought I heard
you come in
as you used to
all the time.

Went downstairs
to look
and saw you walk
through the gate
            smiling.
My head
under your arm
            as usual.

The Launch of a Thousand

I see you sitting out there
somewhere next to me, unaware
you are auditioning for a place
in a life of my choice.
Why me? you say, as we conduct
an imaginary conversation I started,
and signally fail to control
by misquoting Bill Clinton:
It's your cheekbones, stupid!

Sing a song of sex pants

crotchless with a pink bow
viscid are the hairs and thighs
favoured by a tongue

sticking to the bed
Ruby Dick moves under high Cs
keeps an eye out for pantaloons

The Absence of Magic

That conjurers' trick
of love's illusions
would not work
to lift his wand.

Handkerchiefs, up his sleeve,
failed to come forth
on cue, only slipped down
in white shreds upon
the sheets, and no doves
appeared to peck at them.

A Certain Knowledge

i.M. Bob Symes

We talked about your health,
but never your mortality. Often
chatted about football – Crystal Palace
and Fulham. Lunched at The Dorchester,
an eccentric Streatham restaurant you went
to with your mum. Places reserved for regulars,
which kept re-laying to a minimum.
A jug of water on each table, old fashioned
food: meat and two veg, fat chips from before
they became fashionable, crumbles and custard.

After the chemotherapy, the radiotherapy, bone
marrow transplants, all the side effects,
you were sometimes down but didn't succumb,
still managed to come back to life, although
the last decline was the swiftest.
At its beginning, I told you how the science
fiction writer Philip K Dick had to live
with his mortality throughout his time.
When Phillip's baby twin sister died,
their parents had his name engraved

beside hers, left a blank space
to fill, after his date of birth.
You said Dick's early knowledge
must have been terrible to bear. Then
I realised you knew for certain.
In poetry it's said to be right
to follow the rule of three: your first
grandchild, born two months after
Oscar Luke Bob

Ending

Warminster Council wanted to demolish their outside toilet. Peacenik Irene refused, figured she and her husband wouldn't have to think about bungalows, plus the guarantee of fresh air. This paid off, as Jack lived to eighty-four and Irene was eighty-nine when cancer arrived. Driven to a restaurant for her ninetieth, she gave a speech, banged on the table and dished out advice to everyone.

Always maintained she didn't feel any pain but when blood was regularly coughed up, spent two days in Bath Hospital having tests, then decided she'd move into a hospice where family, friends and pets visited. One night, she called nurse Janice over, whispered she needed help to go. Janice told her she'd stay as long as she wished, but first had to leave and inform the on-call Doctor. Irene laughed, explained it wasn't necessary to disturb them, just because she occasionally required some assistance getting to the toilet.

Only Once

I thought that when I saw you
I might fall in love with you again,
and now I have, I know I haven't
– was how my ex-wife Anne greeted me
before we drove from Boston Airport
to her apartment near Brattle Street.

I wanted to say
her response might be coloured
by the fact I'd recently acquired
my worst ever haircut
at the Sassoon Hairdressing School.
How the girl cutting my hair was American
and I so loved her American-ness
as it reminded me of Anne's,
I agreed to her cutting more off
so she'd carry on talking,
but Anne's words silenced me.

I felt better when I saw her books,
familiar from our decade together,
especially LBJ's " Vantage Point ".
She liked Lyndon Johnson –
despite opposing the Vietnam war –
because he had pet beagles like her family's.
It was hard to talk with Anne continually
roller-skating up and down the apartment.
I later realised it was one of the ways
she kept occupied between going to
AA meetings, during early stage sobriety.

When she'd phoned me in London
and confessed to being an alcoholic,
things about our final years together
began to make sense.
Anne had always been a sleeptalker
with eyes wide open as if awake.
This happened more frequently
until she would ask me every night
to check for creatures under the bed.
I'd get up, turn the light on, look,
show her everything was all right.

In the middle of that first night
at her place, I was awoken
by Anne calling out my name.
I got up and stood outside her bedroom.
If she'd called my name again
I would have gone in to her,
but she didn't, so I didn't.
There were no more nights like that.
There were thousands of nights like that.

Reflections at Samos Harbour

As permanent as ice creams,
our reflections in the water
show that if journeys
home have to be made,
they can be made back again,
as easily as ferries here
depart for and arrive from
other islands.

And on some days to come
we may still wave ourselves goodbye,
even if we're going nowhere,
something we learned
as children
after we'd followed the van
with the slow tinkly tune,
whether we were rewarded each time or not.

Accumulation in the Tivoli Gardens

A Japanese pagoda
beside a shaped lake

where big fish gape for food
near a souvenir shop

with lit up Little Mermaids
and swivel Vikings that roar

when drowned by rides
which rollercoast you

as a mother peahen escorts
two tiny mouthful peachicks

towards the corner shelter
of an Art Deco restaurant

their father follows behind
in a vain limelight retreat

Thank you for buying *Krapp's Last Tape*. It is Peter Ebsworth's first poetry collection with us; we hope you enjoyed it. Peter is the founder and current co-editor of the popular South Bank Poetry magazine. He reads his poetry regularly at venues in London – and sometimes further afield.

—§—

the waterways series is an imprint of flipped eye publishing, a small publisher dedicated to publishing powerful new voices in affordable volumes. Founded in 2001, we have won awards and international recognition through our focus on publishing fiction and poetry that is clear and true, rather than exhibitionist.

If you would like more information about flipped eye publishing, please join our mailing list online at **www.flippedeye.net.**

Lightning Source UK Ltd.
Milton Keynes UK
UKHW010721210321
380690UK00002B/93